DEAD AHEAD

BEN DOLLER

Design by   Ben Doller
Author Photo   Don Gochenour

Published in the United States by   Fence Books
                                            Science Library 320
                                            University at Albany
                                            1400 Washington Avenue
                                            Albany, NY 12222
                                            www.fenceportal.org

Fence Books are distributed by   University Press of New England
                                            www.upne.com

and printed in Canada by   Westcan Printing Group
                                            www.westcanpg.com

Library of Congress Cataloguing in Publication Data
        Doller, Ben [1973–]
        Dead Ahead/Ben Doller

Library of Congress Control Number: 2010923756

ISBN 1-934200-35-X
ISBN 13: 978-1-934200-35-3

FIRST EDITION
10 9 8 7 6 5 4 3 2

Grateful acknowledgement is made to the following publications in which the poems in this book first appeared: *Boston Review, The Canary, Columbia Poetry Review, Connotation Press, Denver Quarterly, Electronic Poetry Review, Forklift, Ohio, Indiana Review, jubilat, La Petite Zine, Phoebe, New Orleans Review,* and *Tin House.* "Pan" appeared in *The IE Reader* (Narrow House). "Beret Spotting" appeared in *Satellite Convulsions: Poems from Tin House* (Tin House Books). "The Housesitter" and "Like" appeared in *Short Fuse* (Rattapallax Press).

Thanks, friends.

Fence Books are published in partnership with the University at Albany and the New York State Writers Institute, and with help from the New York State Council on the Arts and the National Endowment for the Arts.

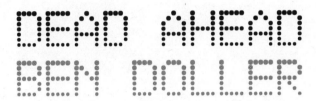

DEAD AHEAD
BEN DOLLER

FENCE
BOOKS

ALBANY

hey Sandra

If I be pitched on for an Expedition of this kinde I would desire to have a Commission as unlimited as might be wth respect to *Time* or *Place* : for in so long a Voyage and an attempt so full of difficulties, 'tis impossible to foresee a thousand Accidents w^{h} may require ye goeing somewhat aside from ye Principall Designe ; and may at the same time offer a yet more valuable Opertunity of some Collaterall Discovery.

—Captain William Dampier

CONTENTS:

What Do You Do

What do you do.

Well. I tie population
knots in a length
of baling twine
laughing at mister
water & my, well—

    (our elation
     ship swell)—

the ratio of life
to rest & a lot

of dogheaded sedans.

Bunny go in your
bunnyhole
then go around you
& go out you
should have known

me before, a human
being being before

a humming bee

kissing all the outlets
the toilets & violets

the various house nozzlets

in every fourth room
there was a stammer in my step
so I had a talking to it
convince it it could & you are it

we worked on our walking til
we made the night air
noisy we worked on our walking
til the soil got glossy

indivisible, with misery, ice
& four owls.

And?

rented a receptacle furnished
with free holes & the spider
in the shower would not look
I crippled it with water
from Le Aquassage
& made its head heavy & so made it fall
glancing off the tile moldy.

One could weave one's
own clothes but might miss
the boxes on the harbor growing
the separate hemisphere boxes
approaching legibility—

but what do you do.

Well. I tie dirty
ribbons round these packages
gift the marble doorsteps
push the bellbuttons & runoff.

Once a sheet of artificial turf
grew inland atop the harbor
I could not walk on that wall
went roughly in.

    (our relation
    ships well)

Before we muttered I had committed
a blunder involving the arbiter
the world series and another
with some other bay

I couldn't help it I heard whale
instructions which turned out
to be emergency emanations
from an abandoned water mine
bobbing undisturbable, with
jittery acoustics, & all.

So. What do you do.

Hell I tie phototropic
cellshards to gulltails
via blowgun shape of
a slogan saying:

"Marry Me Immediately"

dedicated
to the hungry tired
week and the wanting
zones of anatomy
and gut maps

there is a link in your eye
there is a link you can totally
snap your eye

there is the unalienable right to lie
& so on & so what & so forth &

so what if I did or didn't, if I sat here
locating the hugest mote,

I'm alive aren't I.

Pointing Habit

A pointing habit. Over there over there.
Laser pointer. A light, a ray.
A sunhead, shinyeye.
Question of a center, of a question.
But I don't speak semaphore
no more. Gravity can bend it.
A weight.
A stick of space. A beam. Of zilch.
A swivelhead. Reverse trend
in cellular conglomeration. A cult.
An inner target. An origin disorder.
Send the word
send the word.
Telegram. Missile command.
Compulsive pointing. To the point
of meditation. A future gesture.
Black dog lost a yellow tennis ball.
Mission control.
Massive ego.
A grave.
Over there.
A men.
The black dog has lost the tennis ball.
The yellow ball, the dog can't find.
This dog lost that ball.
Infinite finger.
A sunbow. *I threw it | I lost it.*
Such a dandy | No one understands me.
Handshake.
A maniac, pointing.

An inverse church.
A west west east. Hysterical pointing.
Two gloves to a stick.
Fanatic tennis.
The lob. A head. Asunder.
Attendance lesson.
A handgun
and we won't come back
till it's over over there.

On Vacation

honest dust

fraction
of friction

fiction of   are

last then very later

bright dead star

were I were

steadfast as art

or even functioned

or even frisson

—on the front burner molecule flock:—

ice cop

tin come

quick lee

hard lee

whole lee

lee word

world lee

wordly whorled

—is born on back burns wake, prewake or post:
sleep: dreamless, never breathéd death,
never. Never Nothing Nothing, There, we are
going: cold salt sea: see: from the wind
its motes & smoke stem to stern turn there:

the frozenmeat section, here, cold

compressed, unsheathing to beat proteins
vs. verbs: to thaw that kinda christ virus. Out!:

ice cop

(& the sounds of the scraping bowsprit)

tin night

& the sounds of the sounds gone always. Lowdly!)

us sher

(to escort us to our seats, please, sitting on our afts)

use her

(& the interest we earned as we sat there)

ee ting

(the extraterrestrial)

ting ting

(bellesletters)

terrene tinge

(layers for the super scoops)

tinge terrene

(——thend)

honest dust

fashioned
from fusion

fiction of you

sat in the shower stupid

wan, dwarfed, in shoes

were I were

something as art

or even honest

forged with slightly more fire

The Human Experiment

You can picture a trillion go go fields.
On each inch grid a different swab of culture.
Just add light add heat just add water.
But cannot guess what each swab will yield.
When & in which place the plot will rupture.
A conscious bloom that when peeled.
Out will shiver out & search out borders for fire.
Bloom picture the dumb sun circle. Vulture your.
Bald skull skin burns slither to the dirt go shield.
It go dig deep go go where you've already keeled.
[Still shoveling asleep in the finally night] over.
And over it pierced your first & over dream it sealed.
Your eyes open & in them it pitched in them a pasture.

The Housesitter

There are too many
inhalants in the cabinet
in your kitchen

and not enough
bread in your kitchen
but you have barrels of grain

I can grind in the wholesale disaster survival cellar
and
there are enough microrganisms for a month
of leavenings

"cheAlseA BAurunu"

of the few ways your home is like the major whales
one is
I cannot conceive

all of it
just the hotwater heater heating water hotter
the giant screen

its pixel
and oh seven twin kittens
in the box from your printer

milking their mother
who sleeps both incessant
and deeper than any western grave

there are too many paintings
of ledges with nature topping
where the weather is fine and glowing grapes and

the weather surrounds the scoliotic trees
makes one berry biggest
unless you measure

and not enough ottoman
which I feel a significant addition
to leisure machines.

Like

These more recent renaissances
    shall not be attributed to the pains of some few
but rather to the proud ignorances
            of the rest. Those soft sticky things I blew
in your mouth never were summer isis
    but postmortem prepartum dandelion pappus
            parachutes. They will not find purchase

there. We want weeds to burgeon from our mouths
        but from this mouth burgeons only the reek
of the dead things it's eaten. And on the behemoth
            sea off south Florida the sun is passing like
Wallace floating on a rubber innertube,
        full of halitosis, far from accident
or indemnity, he is singing the genius of Haboob

        and Simoon, sandy brothers sifting sand
over his idea of ideal Asia. They grapple in a bout
    about a second then one slumbering wind.
            Hooray for the sun, the imagination, he shouts.
    He shouts, imagined water, hold the sun
and the water breaks in refracted immolation
            and though it blinds him he keeps this song

going. I need not these outer eyes he shouts.
        There are too many songs he shouts.

"Aphorisms are for the appleheads,
Stamped inside a noisy machine——

Maxims for the maniac
We are fashioning a new cliché

Of dither does and camel humps
Of zither plucks on one gross gut of rain."

More song the same. Big man, wee sun.
More womanish, of
perpetual expectation.

To split
the system into lit
& un.

So. Nocturnal emissaries
sleep with moon
in their mouths,

daycreepers swoon
til nine then mar their timecards.
And noon?

Nor.
No mid amidst.
Night and day.

To think you would have had them
be your legacy. To think
at all. Not to.

Supernova, a sloth climbs.
A coconut plops in the water. Goes under.
Over the hills primitives pantomime around a fire.
Light speeds. A bug of a bird. (Commencement day.)

Coco bobs up. The aviatrix oerpassing
looks. Could that be a fishhump. Nope.
Just big seed. Fires in daylight. At the center is
whatever & it's. It's the center, it's it.

Our globe is packed with meat and milk
milt and marrow. Nut catches current,
drifts westward well past sight spinning,
it will not find purchase there, cramped by,

certainly, the sea, nothing without it.
The crown of the ape's head, slick ape paddling
towards the derrick in the distance. Fabulous chimp,
you know how to say hello.

It's 98.6 degrees that's some hot water.
98.6 degrees inside your mother. Speech
lies in our hands, so why cry, mandrill?

Because. I have eaten around.
There is too much delicious.
There are too many songs because.

What is the Opposite of Civilization

the third and only void from the first right
three-celled   transparent cold   crustacean
sweeping   full fathomed floor   night
absolute   under the   i gloo ocean
not   *let there be*   but   gross starlight
calling   this hay   seed in my hand   [quark
of the hayfield   and of the bigger   nouns
it feeds eventualities] this hay seed of a town
out from all   those others   question mark

Maybe   shutting   me maw up not eating
not saying   not kissing nor licking to anoint
the spot   that will permit   me a   meeting
with me   replicate me   exclamation point

Fifteen Minutes

That was easier, one twin said, than it should have been.
Difficult nonetheless.

Yes. The other twin said & Yes.

I said so easy I am offended in fact, though.
I quit to better breathe. I breathed.

Strange how when there is more overhead
there is less to see I said. I meant
more clouds when the moon's not out.

Although said one twin.

What.

Yes what. You said although the other twin said. Although what.

Although. I wouldn't go around telling everyone.
How we were locked inside whatever that was
for howevermany days, whatever, a long long time.
And how we could have broke out this easy
all along but didn't think to do it. How instead
we curled together like a shuteyed litter in the cold dark.
And how finally we smashed it slow, weaker
than we were before for thirst & hungry.

Now it's even colder said the other twin.

Strange how most would think the dark an absence.
What it is is saturation.

Although not that we could. Tell anyone that is.
Except for us. And we know too well I said all this.

There has never been a single silence since the gears
in this motherless earth interlocked then let go then
interlocked so far so good I guess but for awhile
it was what that word silence is for. A silence
with a word for it, a silence while every head
clanged with words for it and plans for it.
Just our breathing & the wind sanding
whatever land it was. Not a silence at all.

Now what do we do one twin said after looking
a long time all of us at the dark.

We should go said one twin. Where said one.
If we knew where we were said one twin
we would know where. We'd go there.

We should have a fire I said. Then we could see
this land look like. And a fire would be warmer.
We could burn what we broke.

It's so cold said one twin.

So whoever put us here could see it & smell it. I think not said
one.

The other one said I also think not. It's so cold.

Twins. Do not travel with twins. Their voices twine
in the dark and perhaps their thinking and you
will be outvoted if you are the only one with them
although they just as often disagree
& they fight & sometimes
there's something extrasensory—
they walk beside with such symmetry,
one's right foot landing on the walk & the other's right raising.
They married different women but on the same day
& each alone together a day later and if you are walking
with them through people people stare & wonder
if you are their odd brother. I myself have wondered.

But I wasn't about to step out into what we were in without
them.

I'm going I said. I'm going and bringing my own warm body.

Slowly we'd begun to feel the sun.

The Breeze

The breeze you breathed

  "you   shouldn't have—
       "

leaving

genially.

My Pirate Novel
    I have so much to yell to you,
  mostly the way the skull

sun hits each soft spot
    of the sea so faithfully so
  solid it makes death one

tense past; tomorrow
    this broth one is steeping in each
  pore stained with seasonings

until the white day
    dilates beyond something you could
  fit in your skull, sun, which

is your novel now.
    Yes and I have to yell to you
  about your characters,

each an orphan, one
    wants something you refuse to say,
  sobbing in his skull ten

men up the mast, sobs:

Land! You were a dream   we could have when it was firm
enough to sleep long enough to dream long enough to sleep
beyond these bodies. But it is a kind of blindness now

for the very   constancy of these   stray waves   the one look
on every   finished face   polished with spray   wettest wood
the tangle of weed spent from the brown sail: same   the same.
Here is the dark   Willy pictured   in blind Skull's   gone eye
dark that may   be a burning   bright for all   the cur knows——

        Then I need to yell into you
   to hold fire, be subtler

now!—keep, if you can,
     that dog's patches over the gash,
the arr-barks, the tri-pegs,

the chewing always
     bloody bullion beneath the floe,
back: forever until

necessary.
    Hesitate to call
these flashbacks, my novel,

just imaginings:
    colonizing an island with
your cannon, coining holiday,

specie, spices, but ever
    finding no island. My Pirate
Novel, each of your actions takes

place, each in your nest,
    nearer to the skull/sun, every
sashed, amputated man

climbs to spy and cry.
      Limbs pile like logs around a stake.
    Each action alone, shone

through a wet glass, not
    one solid step or enemy.
    What, are you called *Downtime*?

Something? Novel, what
      are you, some kind of tragedy?
    But tragedy is unnecessary,

everyone has a
      skeleton to pour rum through, hooks
    for hands, biting money.

No City

But I have no city
no city to call mine

I own no city
nor suburb nor no

fraction of a gate no
but I have no town

no changing train
to own to call to mind

pour me four more
plastic glasses of that stuff

that spits out of the chemistry
sculpture the ingredient

list has the only pretty words
one more glass

like teeth in the entrance

but I have no city
an outline plus stains

a map of trade
routes winds & a market

community a target
humanity niche

I get so twitchy
when they call themselves me

poor wee small & still
sectored into exponential

ampersand halves that we must have
collective & infinitesimally bold

unsleepy really of insignificant massives
made less spectacular by the speed

of the network but we have
the lessons of shad

the congregations at the sopping basis
another full glass of that glass flake

like fangs in the craw

fluoridated they scrape
from cutting room floors

operating room floors
the flooring store

poor us no tv but I guess
I have the movies I guess

full of mistake
cities behind them construction

their own context of powders papers
& fortune the prairies behind them

have their own cities to own
if I had one but the movies

are made to be made
if I made my own city that is

start in the middle & work our way down
shaft of dark lets

for contiguous throngs

> coffee fountains
> cubic fiat
> density dance

but the best thing about a poem
it may be a city or is it a wristwatch

there is always an other

set your bludgeon by it
it all starts with someone

else's colony it all starts with a refusal
a carnal carnival a fun funeral

Prescription Window

Without here

nature or wire,

-(-no, recenter-)-

tsunami tarried

from wearing

bears the fiction

they truly maybe

bombbulged tide,

akin to a map

want to kill her

a brick, or a bag

through atmospheres

lateral motion

like a bumper:

rather within the air still there are shambles but shambles of

of suet in a birdgut shading the spires some moment before

and the shamble of one flashfrozen icelocked thirtystory

in a state of pure antiflux looming over the state she comes

a hat fashioned of knots of twine and stems of weeds only she

of those names of, disfigured as she's made them, disfigured as

are. Strange shadow, circuits of sun strained through the petrified

shadow of contrast-amplified light thread in—glowwormed shade

of the neuromemos of this brain, which make me wonder, lover,

or inversely warn her when something heavy appears for instance

with bricks in it, no, a brick, yes, a brick, no, a block of cinder falls

to her, heads up one might say, or, duck, though neither prefigure

or, contrariwise, to clutch her, absorbing the brunt of the block for her

effect: chivalric affectation: intention: x-eyes.

Much debris and more gravity the further down you go.
dubbed earth daily & person covers person in it when finally they're done
Ping ping. The tidalwave is melting. This month's slow &
vacancies. The livestock may have time to learn
nostrils periscoping the surface like ablated eyes, but do not:
them—we're intolerant—but they keep returning though we've prodded them out
these ancestral pastures, they keep well on grass which is thriving they keep
installed for their exile, groaning then nudging us out of our adequate dream.
Nudge nudge. One toe. One leg on. Blink one bad eye—in prescription window
in foster street lampposts pierce the icewater spilling
from gaslamps. Any two sticks cast a crux in any eddy,
no, two bones cut an intersection at the intersection of two streets,
in perfect parallel like twinning rails retreat into sleep no
sleep is here—leave the driving—the narrower the morrow

Where they meet's
doing, going.
sure, no
to swim & float,
we can't keep
outpast these pastures
rearranging the rootfence
They keep.
a river ascending
sight pools
or an angle, an elbow,
yellow femurs
distance trip—
the merrier the marrow.

Bliss fits.

bliss fits

I'm glad I'm happy.

People are leaving

I believe in beauty

turn, time,

liphinges split.

too much blood

There go their bones.

into the x-ing, knee-deep

clanging lights—

correct & more

concerns & more

ununlike the oneways

Bliss fits that crack in the coolant cube, the calendar crease &

toward the bent backbone or further if further there is.

Prescription window, two brakelights bleed on the wetness you wear.

but slow to go, stopping to let the same train by. And waiting

once, in semiconscious abandon of any notion of space, and in

and thus, us. It was cool but then a yawn so big the skin at my

It's not that it's a perfect bore but that there is *too* much delicious here,

for the lion to rock in. And the gazelles here haven't horns, they're slow.

Then so & so shows, dumps our drinks, flees through the thin yard,

in flood, wild arms. I'd believe again, in some splendid shrieking,

pitched past order, beyond all accounting; judgeless, beyond

toward true, less whatever so and so's latest scalding tantrum

what it is: hemoglobin glowing in half his gangways,

of our marble capital city—same, thing, shrieking, in, the, lights.

For instance I kill

stale plane

now & again

longer than static

even somehow.

doped by the Scum-

ammonia and bleach-

a plump lapis lazuli fly stood on a sliding glass door,

state attached, box of lead humidity scrolling into the ceiling,

heat lightning installs silver shades for smog clots, fixed

cracking itself, shades admitting shape, length, and somehow even,

This time I killed it on my forehead. Early summer,

Buster solvent I used to get protein stains out. Do not mix

may cause coughing, loss of voice, feeling of burning and suffocation, even death.   Do not mix parry and plunge, the

Worse, one may be burned blind. Do not mix

moonshines and breadknives, dueling for the last finger of moonshine.

Shadow, the   gashed fingerpaint against the false fracture of the windowpane.

Do not allow

to set. Do not allow to set for three weeks to a month.

Protein Stains are hard to get out. And I just let my head slip

Mean to. Fragile Buzzing Jewel, now I know you. Wouldn't move. Just kept pushing through,

Close enough to see the contacts.

Fear Death by.

through. Didn't

didn't mean to.

"There was a lot

of blood."

See the mess you've made the mess with your gory eye.

Seems the mess I've made. Something heavy appears for instance
in the Atlantic, the results are in, the test a spectacular mess:
sea swollen: it's armistice day. Peace be with you. You may now
the sign of peace. Or a. Might I suggest the classic embrace,
eyes over each other's shoulder, two in the clock two in the
you in. Timeless fashions, time itself in fact fashioned
or so the planetarium says. They have the night recipe.
to see such little lights. I'm watching you in. You must now desist
zip up your stuff, tie your plant hat back on, stop fogging
or at least let me in. I would like to reduce my preceding suggestion
on the lip, some spit in the eye. Here I am trying fairly hard to skirt
but of course one temptation springs from a lack of attempt, being
beholding in, one can't see for the fog made breathing freezing thick

splitting atoms
water was broken,
offer each other
loins aligned,
window I'm watching
from concussion
It must be dark
this sign of peace,
your window
to a slap
trying here
waist-deep,
on this pane.

No wonder
sharp relief
they installed
I moved here.
wonder. No
on my sentience.
on it. My
Moist as well
The gazelles here,
but big.
come to think
and better, and can
nearly done
you're there,"
And Loose volution?

no one comes around no more. No one calls, photos me in

with the red couch, looking out at the graveyard. No wonder

a graveyard when I wasn't looking. When wasn't I looking? Before

(1673). I think *the neighbors don't give me much trouble*, no wonder no

one polaroids me watching the nature shows, nor do they cheer

I may map it forever. The weather goes sketchy, no one to agree

opinion is the tidalwave has frozen, the shadow we are in is shiny.

misty even, & a gravesite so the super grasses grow. It's easy.

not deserving this exquisite name, are more like guinea pigs,

That's what they're like. A lion can lean on one, nibble as it chooses,

of it, the lions are putting on weight as well. But they think more,

mimic the wheezy, nerveless bleats of the gazelles, who, more like pigs, are

doing. "Approach, gazelles, come, come out I see you at least I know

the lions are like. Close the curtains, turn the window off.

Well push my barque in the water & blow it to the cross-tops

Sin is sound but what is sound now that sin's been said

servos bring the ground to her. The system is a shroud

the system is a shroud that soaks the weaker weather

bell is a golden goblet. I heard them call it a Grail.

cabinet's filled with lachrymal she drinks it deep

then she strikes it with her tail can I run from the shade

shade which she wants but she hid it I can't find it

help I can see it all at once. Four factors forged

frost   filth   fuel   flame)

looking glass, I see right through it and still cannot tell a lie

from fact or truth or simple song. It's an aquarium

where alchemicals swim like stingrays. It's an aquarium

where I am bubbling in my brass suit among this false fauna.

I am, a sucker swabbing the glass for food with my face—

it's an aquarium, the water risen head high, a cataract

Without

Within. Her

Her

Within

out here

Without her

Within her

Within here

in here

in Here

out here

Within

Beret Spotting

The other other afternoon only after
a hearty brunch of nectarine squab,
scrambled eggwhites & wet toast,
coffee juice grapefruit juice & port,
a fine cake of air & sweet spindles,
a nap on the prototypical orange
square did I realize there was still time.

Coughdrops, trillennia. Umm, spirals:
there was still time for beret spotting:

so I hoofed down the bony boulevard
toward the hectic esplanade.

My prior imbibing cost me my good breath.
—Nothing kills me how the hiccups kill,
trust, if manufactured and implemented
as torture, had I a state, or a secret,
I would blurt them quick as the mention—this
from one who would happily test the
Punishing Shoes or the Heretics Fork for

just a second. Or even the Head Crusher,
minus the skull-steadying spike. Maybe even the Iron Maiden

or the Judas Cradle. Perchance the Hard Rock. Forget about
the Rack, the Pear, the Boots, the Saw, and the Wheel.

I'll have none of the monosyllabic devices.

"Launois *et al.* collected the words for hiccup
in 23 languages. Many, but not all of them,

are onomatopoetic. In English at least,
the sound of a hiccup and the burp it produces are
considered embarrassing but there is no help for it."

Since there is no help, come let us piss & fart
"A hiccup is essentially an abrupt Mueller maneuver.
The glottis closes to prevent inspiration

35 milliseconds after electrical activity rises above the baseline in
the diaphragm and external intercostal muscles"

Were it not for my glottis closing, I may never
have spasmd upon the trail of crayons.
For I seldom watch the ground walking, but,
so convulsd, noted there were crayons there.
Poor child, to hoof alone that path
humping a 64-pack still fresh,
unstained by the complete page, unstained Flesh

(since '62, *Peach*)
unstained Melon, Maize, Green-Yellow,

unstained Salmon, Thistle, Yellow-Green,
unstained Raw Sienna, Hot Magenta,

unstained Black. White. Unstained Gray.
Poor child, the path to you melts
in radiant pools, in a sun the same
as yesteryear's. I thought. I thought

what you thought I'd think: "I must
find you. Whatever if the wax stains my shift,
whatever calico." You know, I began to follow
gathering wickless crepe-wrapped tallows.

Your trail fell behind the arc that the world is.
Incidentally a very meager world one day only.

Forty-four colors to the azure, cerulean, very pretty sky.
Which, incidentally.

I followed, you were nowhere found to be.
Nay, I have done, you get no more of me.
But these flowers where which I got lazy
are there. I there, locked looking. Spamm'd
again. So delicate and damp the physiological individuality
despite the scores of scores in near facsimile
hooded reddening bulbs sweet spindles.

"How do they survive the bigtime wind?"
"They don't have to, this is an asylum."
Which explains, I suppose, why I spot no berets.

Pan

Ellie Mannette, Inventor

just bang this steel haste that sound
just breathe this straw oscillation

barely bend steel compost 2 more
bunch more straws hotwax scald that a scale

1 end will crook back bow here
short high straw to choose w/ my 40
hooves

these 3 will weave the garrote cord
the throat of straw all warm air

soon a song steel be struck in the round
syrinx hear you are out straw wind where you
waste

from your throat metal a real gusher goes there if
I have a hammer

/A WOLF TONE/

syrinx the midwife made shrieks at my straw
beard

panic
deliverer

it's vast trash it's metal melt down & absolutely free

already we know that 1 straw song already

unlike sound you chose not to be steel
                              unlike sound compost straw heap
                    the cane can   who can?
                         play the hurricane

     big steel can in the water big united states navy can
straw in the pond in the straw eating wind

                    dark metal swim
                       esophagus party
                                   hit it violins

steal it on your metal bike stomp it to the chrome house
        handlebar metal tubular steel 55 gallon man

        can't have skin skin's too   can't have tamboo bamboo
              it might be a langwage a riot

                    it may be
                    too too

             get back Apollo!
                    (you buffet)
        move over rover

        the best lyrists smash their lyres
                    the very make them fire

        if midas likes it it must be bullion
anything that breathes is okay ok

I say shoot anything that breathes ok
                        just change the names

Shell Invaders

Esso Tripoli

Amoco Renegades

The Widow Ching Poems

But the battle did not begin. The sun rose peacefully and without haste set again into the quivering reeds. The men and the arms watched, and waited. The noontimes were more powerful than they, and the siestas were infinite.

—Borges

But most miracles are very bad.

Don't remind me.
Remind me
telepathically or in spine-
signs or in. Remind me
later, in dialectic seizure.
In strings of fives
tallying days inside.

What storm is this story
what shape has all these names.

Remind me of the hold in the hold.

We were holding an emergency
on the quite long side of a green gate
or an intervention.

I promised I would bite
out the sun's white part:

just change your name.
I will eat every organ.

There is the miracle of the opening eyesore,
the white field paved long before you

were there, the field raining. Sheet lightning
in the pinhole. Storm-swell in the big nerve.

And when we kindled the coastals,
they went deep in & seeded the steppes.

Master of the Royal Stables, I tried it out.

You sure got cut by the catamaran,
cut bad. I do not have what you have
why should I take what you take.

Bad rice.
Dead greens.
Dog rain.

Rain cues a cart of sods,
new weeds pushing out new weeds.
Roots in the muck of the slow decompose.

Remind me of the wooden acrobat posed
in the elephant's nose one leg perpendicular
toes stained the chartreuse color.

Hands stained seagreen.
A smarter monster. A head.

I am 40,000 alone.

There was really no progress
ever made on the basic boat.

Which reminds me now like certain scent:
holeblack peat, where the seed goes,
the seed, where the stem goes, the stalk
and the shell.

The way what they used to call censored
makes the weeds to grow, fronds flare,
fronds fill the big bay, fronds fix
in the oarlocks of our basic, semi-abandoned
boat, with a man and a woman
impersonating sleeping, balanced
atop a—for these purpose—a bottomless.

There is not enough time enough, nor world.
Perhaps world enough. Not time enough though.
There is not enough enough, nor enough time
enough to tally. But if still the sun could reason

with the rest it allows

with the digital dragon.

Which reminds me of a curtain sound:

 aches that throat that makes that red cloud.

We were favoring one side like an obelisk
in the shallow cave shade. An obelisk
obviously made for living.   Halloo!
What's the average color down there?

I don't know. Neither do I. I do, but I can't tell you.

Me too. I'd love to tell you but I can't
tell you enough.

white wave

yellow label

green ensign

red rag

purple pennant

black bunting

A coin. A rock.

a rock-coin. A rock
I skipped
thrice across
the swollen sea
when I found you
wearing a hole.

A coin my eyes wear so as
not to surge north.

A rock I worked a hole into
to tie a rope to me
to skip into the green sea.

The miracle

the chain of accident
accident emits
the miracle of a stray shot
entering the window
of the parlor
exiting the window
of the kitchen

allowing the woodsmoke out.

The vixen seeks the wing.

One morning that's all that
that whole day.

Then & finally
I Shall be Some
Body Else.

I Should Send You
off alone
in our own sure skiff
You, your stagnant blood

the sea shrugs
stacked flags.

The sea takes.
Galleon blood.

I was water once well beyond.
So was I. Me
too. Point A,
where things
send sends from, starved
loudly. Me
too.

Was where the formula goes.
Unlike a stone.
We have not met enough.

Which reminds me enough
enough
of the song cast
in the nod of the one
playing her silver behind the kitestrains
of yellow stormlife.

Shall I sing
(I rarely sing)
of the patina
of promotion
the name unlike the name
that going
(everywhere)
you gave

green

the promotion
that came relinquishing the fleet

The Lustre of True Instruction.

Sunk enough.

Sun enough.

There is sea enough.

And space.

There is just now

flood enough

to take.

Speaking of the Ploughman

Earthherder, the onus is
on you anyway. You look at it
once it's gone. It's gone.

Black spears are in the ground.
Looking's alright, I suppose,
but the skewered bones, the—

Earthherder, the weather around
you: irony, and a failing metal, escaping
the planets & the planets' 365 moons.

So, this is what cold could be.
Eventually a husk will grow if
only you stay uncomfortable.

So stay, grow one—
gowns alone are not to be worn
in these wind piles.

You are not that much more insatiable
now than you will be in a song
your child if you make it live may say:

how you left when leaving was honorable,
warm milk cooling sure on a snowy pile.

But the skewered bones.
Rusty scimitars probe froze
manure. Ploughman, base, acid in one.

A baby could do that, but a baby didn't.
A seed in your stomach could erupt into an orchard
anytime, but a seed didn't.

This is so morning. An ice age, lonely.
This is so snowing, something to swallow
something to make a man of.

column.

this is a column that cannot connect
marble floor or entablature, that lacks
both base and capital, it bears no frieze
of perpetual arrangement chiseled
into all night, it is not night it bears
no sky at all, no age, it stands all shaft,
child of the inexhaustible circle
& fixed segment, fragment & fire, it turns
bearing & bearing no load, our unset
cylinder but with set sides from this side
one tallies ten on one's hands, understanding
ten more, do I harbor Doric order,
this column cannot connect completely
to any eye, it recedes to a line
that sets going an endless string of sides,
it ends and returns again, set in no
soil it spins if you are willing to say
so, do you like circumferences going
do you prefer return, this column could
be a concrescence, this this, flecked column
that could be a spine though a spine that can
not connect heads or walkers, minute spine
whose synapse must be advanced by its guests,
vandalized or inscribed by its sculptors:
"it is gone but it left its glitter here"

(cont'd later) "it's back but wore no glitter"
"a penis is not a poem, a pen is"
igneous, I think this spine is or may
be amalgamate this column is but is
isn't a good verb now is it, I heard
a word is best served by that which it isn't,
a conglomerate of differences this
column is, not a hawksbill turtle beak
in a sponge, not dumptruck nor her glitter,
not Rome or Montpelier or some other
column even, not parachutes falling
away from every other thing, not fall,
no, this column is not glitter it bears
no resemblance, it bears no earth, no work
was done to erect it, it has not been
erected, no, this column cannot be
copied though it is a copy itself,
it is not itself, it is not about
nor about to open, well it could be
a spine it has been said if you say so,
depends on what your definition of
could be could be; I like it enough, I
hate it as much, at least it isn't some
kind of message, if only it was, at
least it has rudimentary symmetry

on its side to keep it from thinking too
wide, it bears no thinking it is not that
kind of spine, a pen is a column that
can, would the visitors bring pens they could
scribe its side, o it is 0 & 1 is
it not, it is everything between, is
that everything, surely it has to be
a rod with two ends where it gets cut off
-you said there are ten sides not one didn't you
-age has ground the edges down I said twenty
-you said this column bears no age didn't you
-it is possible I was wrong perhaps
it bears the age of its silent guests who
are its sculptors but those are differences,
this is a column that cannot connect
either human, it just kind of stands there,
if it looks like eleven it's a lesion,
ingenious, I think this spine is or may
be not, there's not much color there is there,
there is no sun, this column's been scratched out
in black & white, no, yes & no, siren
& silence this column is as concrete
as it can, it has stripped the land it came
from, circular but not reciprocal,
it climbs down or up to its quarterpoint,

morphine and phoneme, a simple machine
lever, wheel, pulley, incline, wedge & screw
there are things it could do but it doesn't
know how to or know, it screws no heavens,
it levers no grave, it alludes only
to itself if you say so it has no
self, it is hard to tell if this column was
formed or lathed, if the former the trowel,
the latter the blade, if the former the
future, the latter the yore, the former
supposes moisture, the latter glitter
dust & sand but there are signs of neither
element circling in storms around it
around it is nothing which is pretty
quiet, it would refuse to be news had
it will to refuse, still it refuses
in its sculptor's nerves, little spine that
just can not catch can, can not catch cannot,
it should catch, it is a hundred hands high,
a hundred spans, unregistered structure
where nothing can live, it has no core be
it hollow or hard, fragment or fire, an
edifice where nothing can die, nothing
is spared its sheer redundancy because
this is a column that cannot connect

The Great Fig

(*Museum Natural History/Glass Plants*)

Behold the ancient elastic community,
motion detectors stunned by the sanitary
frantics of the touch addicts.

Behold the obvious mask classic,
feathery pitch locked with small bugs, lipstick
or water clumped from soft rock.

I, I have so many many, I have
so many with me: earlike ovary
of the great fig; umbrella skeleton.

Behold the forest pig & sea cow conspiring
in the shallows, shaded by the scoliotic woods.
They conspire for me. They're disgusting.

The crew team cannot hear me above their rowboat.
They are so dry. All astride their stuttering sea horse.

O to be so very very, to be so very missing
but not to be missed from the terrible story
of which kid got lost in the scoliotic woods.

To be just half-crazy: all, all adornment, all spiral, or square.
Behold the Bent-Hearted-Bride of the Itchy Wharf,
her whole bouquet. She must increase herself.
behold the man from the town, freshly bastarded.

The town or the man? We must increase himself.
A flower is blown. Behold this brown-blown flower.
Drop it not. Host no decrease, into many shining pieces.

Behold, I must increase myself. Behold the Pittsburgh
of the human body through the Venus-eyetrap,
the pond of Visine and the glass lake I spit where
we shall live once and ere in your glass palm steaming.

Bayonet

best then to be the bayonet
slugs hot in the first row

of men will not
be dug out again

bestkept deathclose
at hand more human

hand learnt to hunt
previous the thumby tongue

best only then to be the bayonet
to prick it painter to an end

perfect breathing word
or merely a generous maim

the approximation of blood
hand hunts the water

two stones to rub to gather
not for fire for one stone soft

enough to shape to murder

feed   only then fire

one soft stone enough
to slay & then & only say

new breaths they waft
flesh long sounds hunt

hounds caught hung
in their master's own hunty webs

it is so night sky
stabbed to a quarterlight

the smoke crumpled
the cries   the captives

bandaged in their pens
read the book we gave them

each took their slit page
or took the halfsleep

of the beaten/maimed
one could cut a card

of wheat with this
net all the real vowels in it

nearby a millwheel one might
perform a tracheotomy

no matter which is better
best to best one

Porch

Brazenly, crazilily, now activate the buzzer
which utilizes magnetism to summon

vibrations or sounds this summer
one cannot hear so depth

entrenched in this house you're no
affiliate though the finger fits,

though one light pops on beneath
pinker lunula redder bed

instead of scurrying now stand
jammed in it for much of a minute bending

the first distal phallange nearly into
the first letter in *Letter*, one of which

you're not here to deliver, no message
either—just this white patch flower

stomped unraveling the numbers
on the official belly of a camo chopper.

Paint, paint it cobalt or at least black
pock, pock some stars in it, like lizard,

dolly, dolly it up like a stormcloud,
its very engine nature, its very buzzer

nature, like that sun you shave drip
fire on our third-best small city,

on the pillars of flowers, on the lone
cracked corsage here to pin to a person,

would one answer, oh, and by all
means lose the thirtytwo, the trouble

is you think the trouble is such sway
should be assignable while preferred

stray gods stay blind, we might pry
in the thorn, pop the eye not to note

the feasible so abridged & so defined,
abstruse terrestrial, shush riot sky.

Nice porch somewhere between
a tight place & ether major, triples

as vestibule, *no stynkyng flesshe*
myth in the poorche abyde, breeze

puffs, cut sunny steps, hanging
baskets, earthenware urns full of dirt

& great plants shiver & change
shade bred to feed only pretty bugs

pine grid, stapled, whitewashed, spackles
the spaces with day rhombs, perfect

latticework, plots the distance, props
ivy vines & wings danger danger chair

hangs eye-hooked to the canopy, day
hangs now hello hidden, I did it in,

the beast in the arrangement, presenting
avalanche, inundation, the first person.

Period Style

The rays of light differ from those of invisible heat only in point of period.
—TYNDALL

Camera birdseyeing a pan of beefstuff,
Cooking with Ali, why don't you fog up?
Fingers pinch in parsley color—color

comes but in just the hundred spots scattered,
skin conditions, once folded in the herb
is virtually illegible, vapor

braids by in orders angelic. Gravy:
drippings + ground grain + wrung teat [savvy
chefs would do to use a thick-bottomed pan

with good heat distribution qualities,
otherwise the starch granules in the
roux cook too quick] + some aromatic plant

such as basil, thyme, rosemary [parsley
if that's all you've got], optional. Birdseye,
is not your oculus an obstruction

to Ali?—we have a better view of
the simmering than she, though she fired up
the flame and lowered it in her blow-dried

safety hair, her year-long collection of
smart aprons emblazoned with pictographs—
today's a smiling sun frying face-side-

up in its own skillet: incredible
apocalypse: ecstatic; edible.
The albumen's a ten-pronged corona.

Ten prongs, like a hand-forged clam rake, Yimou's
new martial-arts film, *Shi Mian Mai Fu*,
bodhisattva Vajarasatava's

Vajra: a meditation thunderbolt,
or THE TINGLER, a copper hand that
offers the ultimate in head massage—

slide the phalanges slow over the crown
& feel the shivers of relaxation
over your body or a friend's body!

There's even a pet version! Mid 19th
c. eggs, deyolked, thinned + iodine
switched to froth & fallen, were next applied

to glass plates to make the image adhere:
nothing can be easier than to smear
plates for taking views of ruins, sometimes

defects in the spreading of albumen
create positive beauties in depictions
of negative, black-daubed skies.

More challenging to coat the plates evenly.
It can be done. If the manipulation
of the albumen is well managed,

the picture is more satisfactory
& truthful than when tried with collodion
or paper. By these latter processes

the sky is so dense that when printed it
leaves the paper clean & clear, the result
is a white washed wall, not the appearance

of distance & air. In such photographs
there is no "bridal of the earth & sky"
but rather an all-embracing divorce.

Albumen is too sluggish to imply
moving clouds, but it invariably
presents the sensation of sky & air.

What positive beauties bright dead stars are,
hurling their shrapnel like white-hot murders
of burning blackbirds into sweltering
igloosfull of part-time astronomers.

What negative beauties their dark scars are,
void in a void, unavoidable, ring
of the bride who went so fat they severed
her finger, nothing lives save the Cheshire

frown of a light beam bent to ablation
& then beyond, to ablated, even
to late, too late. 0 are you further
divisible are you the divisor?

Ali, Ali, Oxen-Free.
Eli, Eli, lama sabachthani.

Ali Ali Oxen Free
Eli, Eli, lama sabachthani.

Come out come out wherever you be.
My lord my lord why have you forsaken me?

Echo o no can't see
dimension devotion to voce or

visage besottoed, unseen//
unsent, swear unsworn—

cameraman
0 the history

gossip of the ability
to observe

the wight, the white, the wit, the weight, the way—
the night, the nit, the not, the note, the neigh

borealis, I know how the heifer goes:
moo, the oxen must go more like a horse
the oxen like to be free, they shout nay.
Nay, the air sings hissing twinks of their chains.
Toro. Both are branded their constellations,
punctured. The molten freedom of money!
Orion aims no shaft or string at light-eras
of quiet (great target)—how many stacked brains
supply that fine flesh, the horse's downy
wings? Yes & faith in the god's mistakes:
they kill everyone, some few they position
astride the cosmos, terrific distance
between their joints—void—commemorating
the thing they do that makes them what they are.

That thing they do to tell us who they are?
—Style, *black-clad solitude that is not sad.*
So the true hunt is in the aim, aye?
                                    Dear Dad,
now I know why you never patented
your best invention yet: *a revolution*
in our relationship with the dearly departed,
your plaques: *composite of cremated cadaver*
& a chemical colloid that produces an emulsion
as hard as stone, & that, once styled, engraved,
lasts longer than the wall from which it is hung—
new wings were installed in the thing in your head,
more wings (*there's even a pet version!*)—
I know why, besides that name (*Plaquetypus*™) your
shop still teems with the dust of the unclaimed dead,

still reeks with the must of the unclaimed dead,
though not the incense of your departed mother.
But there are pictures on the walls of her
on the border of becoming something other.
Pictures of her smiling in a sun-hat before
the silver box composed of digital shutters
you hold against your camera head.

The stone had a space for the chiseled script
reserved.
My style is to bring in a machine as soon
as it might mean, & yours is to build one
from the husks of some other totaled ones.
Your fleet of dismantled Z-280's, Datsuns.
Style makes the man go on. At ninety-one,
she drove every Friday to have her hair done.

Every Friday she drove to have her hair done,
every Friday to the minute, through snow
& fog. Warm up the Nova & go on.
When your hair is done, you go. Let the wind drone
& roil it feral from its Aqua Net
why should it hold. Then let it freeze again.

It's done. You'll catch your death, hurry——get
in your Nova & go on. The weatherwoman
has a hundred ways to say there's yet
another week of this infernal frozen
meteorology: anenometer,
barometer, conductivity meter, doppler…

it covers the war but will not stick. It "blankets."
What to see when sun & moon have set?

What do you see? The sun & moon have set:

—Zodiakos kyklos, false dawn, precession
of the equinox cannot quit breaking—

cannot quit breaking merely
                            into delay

cannot quit breaking
                        into beginning,
into
        full
        (or full gone) day—

breaking, breaking, beginning & beginning
to break into beginning then beginning
to break again.

Ermine, must you,
you must, mark yourself a moment
between bronzed ground & sleet blast,
(cameraman has yet to catch it)
color of a cracked compass,

color of a mad cloud?

Must it, me musket-heart, diastole
                            oncet?—

born to close,

                cannot quit breaking—

Fix it.

Fix it. Fix it. Fix
it. Fix it—

Now I know how to fix a Blakean Fishpie,
So-called because the vivid yellow of
the saffron-tinted sauce reminds me of
one of those gorgeous sunbursts. The saffron adds
significantly more than depth of colour:
it headily redeems the cottonwooly,
insipid fillets that are sold in plastic-clad
polystyrene trays at the supermarket;
useful when you can't get to a fishmonger.
Ali, how not to be zero's doppelganger?
Headily redeem me, please, headily blend
me with saffron or something equally
salacious & fine, I seek simply the supplies
to draw space clearly, to stay within the lines.

To draw space to me, to stay within my lines
I seek merely the gravity of lead,
but lead that's boiling gold & gaining speed
in a cauldron made of nothing but solar shine—
glass canon, astigmatic Hubble glare,
how is the sun dialed in, is the stone scratched?
Morning, how you want your eggs done?—crackt.

And what will scrape the bays of a tame cur
from Voyager's gold-plated records,
how will our extraterrestrial DJ cue
the 55-tongue salute (Akkadian to Wu)?

Will it be sad? Will it have vocal cords
to howl along with? Will it depress pause,
bored, at last, knowing how the cipher goes?

Why don't you fog up? Even Ali wipes
her glasses dry on her apron sometimes,
& she is the centerpiece—no, she's *with*,

her own cooking's sidekick, the alchemy
itself plays the lead—no, we already
recognize what's about to happen: post-

third-commercial-break: out of the oven
the preprepared version shall be summoned,
more perfect than any process, you almost

wish they wouldn't eat it, crack open the beast
the same way they used to in the 18th
c. —let Ali take you on a journey

deep into culinary history,
a people are only as strong as the
muscles & plants they eat [cue drum & fife].

From this position I have learned how to
crystallize fruit; to make invalid soup;
salmagundi; & now to roast a boar

over the coals of a ransacked house
[portrayed by pig & propane grill of course]
with a gravy you cannot stop stirring

until every fleck of flour fades from taste
into sky or air & gathers someplace
not this zero lens. Cooking, then, is life

["cooking lives—" one apron says] that which pastes
itself ["—cooks die"] to the transparent glass:
motion, or what is made of it behind

the eye? Perhaps this would explain the ducts—
the bridle from sky to earth is rain, truck-
loads of freezing, falling floods, filthy rain

fallen, fingering the copper casket
(having freed the tarp), breaching the gasket,
finding her still unburied, negating

her makeup with googols of gluoned coils,
overflow then overflowing the hole
they dug for her just before it began

to rain, permeating an adjacent
wall, then fondling her husband, so patient
these fifteen years, so patient he's begun

to dust, now to mud & gush & boil
through the seams of his out-moded model
finding newborn streams between the stratum

periods troweled, then injected into streams
the eye may keep, at last—not finally—
to sea, baked back to sun. What reduction!

What sogged cycles! Yet another bridal,
invisible, from earth to sky, suicidal
centaur with no substantial bough to string

itself from, insufficient throat & nostrils
for bodies & limbs so strangely vital
only crossbred faith & math can begin

to explain the breathing of the machine
to the machine. Would someone please explain
it to me? Does Nova know? I'd Tivo

it & watch a solar system explode
repeatedly, set in some brand-new mode
that steadily speeds frame motion from slow

to breakneck until vibration. I'll pause
a few times a moment before there was
nothing left. It's before. There's nothing left.

Each Thing Charged

Each thing, charged
with ought, bends—

breaks light, which
is ought but

part star. Ought
is, I see

in the thick
book, a vulgar corruption.

Someone heard
someone say

an aught when
they said a

naught. Each thing,
charged with a

naught, bends,
breaks light bad.

I am not
a vulgar corruption.

Let's play oughts
and crosses

in this tree
time is not

a line. You
blocked me with

your cross. Cat
wins, random fortunate cat.

The tree bleeds
the blood gums,

blubs, positively
Butterworth.

—*My* head, it
ought to have

a cap like
that, yellow,

threaded, and
all. Each thing

ought to too
the stars are contagious.

Ben Doller is the author of two previous books of poems: *Radio, Radio* (LSU Press, 2001, selected for the 2000 Walt Whitman Award from the Academy of American Poets by Susan Howe), *FAQ:* (Ahsahta Press, 2009). Doller co-edits the Kuhl House Contemporary Poets series from the University of Iowa Press and was recently hired as Assistant Professor in George Mason University's MFA program in Creative Writing. He lives with his lady, Sandra Doller, and their animals.

Fence Books supports writers who might otherwise have difficulty being recognized because their work doesn't answer to either the mainstream or to recognizable modes of experimentation.

The Motherwell Prize is an annual series that offers publication of a first or second book of poems by a woman, as well as a one thousand dollar cash prize.

Fence Books also publishes the Fence Modern Poets Series. This contest is open to poets of any gender and at any stage of career, and offers a one thousand dollar cash prize in addition to book publication. Fence Books is also a participating publisher in the National Poetry Series.

For more information about the first two prizes, visit www.fenceportal.org, or send an SASE to: Fence Books/[Name of Prize], SL 320, University at Albany, 1400 Washington Avenue, Albany, NY, 12222.

For more about *Fence,* visit www.fenceportal.org.

FENCE BOOKS

THE MOTHERWELL PRIZE

Living Must Bury   Josie Sigler
Aim Straight at the Fountain and Press Vaporize   Elizabeth Marie Young
Unspoiled Air   Kaisa Ullsvik Miller

THE ALBERTA PRIZE

The Cow   Ariana Reines
Practice, Restraint   Laura Sims
A Magic Book   Sasha Steensen
Sky Girl   Rosemary Griggs
The Real Moon of Poetry and Other Poems   Tina Brown Celona
Zirconia   Chelsey Minnis

FENCE MODERN POETS SERIES

Duties of An English Foreign Secretary   Macgregor Card
Star in the Eye   James Shea
Structure of the Embryonic Rat Brain   Christopher Janke
The Stupefying Flashbulbs   Daniel Brenner
Povel   Geraldine Kim
The Opening Question   Prageeta Sharma
Apprehend   Elizabeth Robinson
The Red Bird   Joyelle McSweeney

NATIONAL POETRY SERIES

The Black Automaton   Douglas Kearney
Collapsible Poetics Theater   Rodrigo Toscano

ANTHOLOGIES & CRITICAL WORKS

Not for Mothers Only: Contemporary Poets on Child-Getting & Child-Rearing
Catherine Wagner & Rebecca Wolff, editors

A Best of Fence: *The First Nine Years,* Volumes 1 & 2
Rebecca Wolff and *Fence* Editors, editors

POETRY

The Sore Throat & Other Poems	Aaron Kunin
Dead Ahead	Ben Doller
My New Job	Catherine Wagner
Lake Antiquity	Brandon Downing
Stranger	Laura Sims
The Method	Sasha Steensen
The Orphan & Its Relations	Elizabeth Robinson
Site Acquisition	Brian Young
Rogue Hemlocks	Carl Martin
19 Names for Our Band	Jibade-Khalil Huffman
Infamous Landscapes	Prageeta Sharma
Bad Bad	Chelsey Minnis
Snip Snip!	Tina Brown Celona
Yes, Master	Michael Earl Craig
Swallows	Martin Corless-Smith
Folding Ruler Star	Aaron Kunin
The Commandrine & Other Poems	Joyelle McSweeney
Macular Hole	Catherine Wagner
Nota	Martin Corless-Smith
Father of Noise	Anthony McCann
Can You Relax in My House	Michael Earl Craig
Miss America	Catherine Wagner

FICTION

Flet: A Novel	Joyelle McSweeney
The Mandarin	Aaron Kunin